I Wish, I Wish

Paul Shipton

Illustrated by John Eastwood

OXFORD
UNIVERSITY PRESS

1

'Something for nothing'

Debbie counted out the money for the tenth time. It didn't add up to much, even with the money from her old piggy-bank and the coins she had found down the back of the couch. One pound and thirty-four pence, to be exact.

'You should look after your money,' said her sister, Vicky. 'Save up, instead of buying things you don't need.'

Vicky was full of sensible advice and Debbie always found it useless.

You could get a job...
like me.

Vicky did a paper-round every morning and every afternoon. Every week she put the money away in a savings account.

Debbie liked the idea of having money, but she didn't like the idea of earning it. Getting out of her nice, snug bed on wet and windy mornings? Yuck!

She said, 'There isn't *time* for me to get a job. Not before Mum's birthday. And I'll never get her a good present with *this* much money.'

Vicky looked up from her homework.

Vicky shrugged. 'You can't get something for nothing,' she said.

Debbie let out a sigh. Her sister was right – she'd never be able to afford a nice present. But then an idea hit her. There was a second-hand shop on the High Street. She would be able to find a present there, even if it wasn't brand new. *After all*, she told herself, *it's the thought that counts*.

Twenty minutes and a speedy bike ride later, Debbie was standing inside the second-hand shop.

It was cramped and gloomy, and it was packed full of all kinds of things – old tables and chairs, rusty bike frames, and old photos. Some of the stuff looked okay, but most of it … well, 'junk' was the word that popped into Debbie's head.

What's more, there were no price tags. Debbie had no idea which things she could afford. The man behind the counter didn't rush to help – he sat there, as still as a statue, reading his newspaper.

Debbie was starting to think this hadn't been such a good idea after all… And then she saw it.

It was a small brass lamp. It was old and battered – *that's because it's an antique*, Debbie told herself, *and Mum loves antiques*. She picked it up carefully. It was perfect – or at least it *would* be perfect once it had been cleaned up. But did she have enough money to buy it?

Er, how much is this?

The man's eyes flickered up from his paper for an instant.

'One pound, thirty-four pence,' he said.

Debbie couldn't believe it – that was exactly how much money she had! It was a sign – this was the right present to buy.

2

Mr Bloodmoney

Debbie put the lamp carefully into the basket on her bike – she didn't want to bash it up any more on the ride home.

She was about to set off, when a big, fast car pulled up outside the shop. No, make that a HUGE fast car.

A thin-faced man in a long coat stepped out. He was followed by a big man in a suit and mirror-sunglasses (even though it wasn't sunny). *He must be a bodyguard*, thought Debbie.

The two men marched into the shop.

I never knew people like that came to second-hand shops, thought Debbie with a shrug. Then she hopped on her bike and started pedalling home. She couldn't wait to show Vicky the lamp.

She had only been riding for a few minutes, when she heard a beeping horn behind her. It was the same big car. It overtook her and screeched to a halt. Debbie only just managed to brake in time.

The rear window slid slowly down and the thin-faced man leaned out.

The man gave a thin-lipped smile. It didn't set Debbie's mind at rest. 'My apologies,' he said. 'Jenkins, my driver, is sometimes a little too… keen. Let me introduce myself – my name is Charles Bloodmoney.'

His smile widened and Debbie saw all his teeth gleaming. It made her think of a crocodile.

Of course, she knew that she should not talk to strangers and she was about to cycle away.

But then Bloodmoney said:
'You must be wondering why we stopped you... Well, for many years I have been looking for ... something. This morning I was told that I might find it in a second-hand shop. I went there as quickly as I could. But I found that it has just been sold... to you.'

So that was it – the lamp! This Bloodmoney wanted the lamp!

Debbie shrugged. 'Oh well, better luck next time.'

Bloodmoney's eyes were cold. 'I'm afraid you do not understand. The lamp is not valuable in terms of money, but it has great *sentimental* value to me. I want that lamp and I am willing to buy it from you.'

Sorry— it's not for sale.

Not even for— £100?

Debbie let out a gasp. Had she heard right? One hundred pounds! It was incredible.

She took the lamp out of the basket, ready to hand it over. But then she saw the twinkle of greed in Bloodmoney's eyes and a new thought jumped into her mind: *Hold on! Maybe it's worth MORE than £100 – much more?*

She shook her head.

Bloodmoney's voice got louder and there were two little red spots of excitement on his pale cheeks.

Debbie didn't know what to say. A thousand pounds was a lot of money, but maybe this lamp was worth even more. Maybe it was a priceless antique? There was something about Mr Bloodmoney that Debbie didn't trust.

She shook her head one more time and the smile on Bloodmoney's face vanished. He fixed her with a glare as cold as a fish's and shouted to the other man inside the car.

The big man in the sunglasses leapt out of the car and rushed towards her.

He was fast, but Debbie was hard to beat on a bicycle. She tossed the lamp back into the basket, and was already pedalling away down the road. She heard the big man huff and puff as he tried to keep up with her on foot.

She heard the car roar into life again. It wouldn't take long to catch up with her. But there was a footpath ahead – no car could follow her along that. If she could only make it there...

She forced her legs to go faster. Behind her the roar of the engine was getting louder. The big car was getting closer and closer. Nearly there...

Just before the car caught up with her, Debbie swerved onto the footpath. She was safe! Behind her she could hear the angry blare of the car's horn and a howl of rage from inside the car.

She cycled home as fast as she could.

3

The secret of the lamp

Debbie couldn't wait to tell Vicky all about the lamp, but her older sister had already left for her afternoon paper round. There was no one else at home.

She carefully put the lamp on the kitchen table. It didn't look very special, but Debbie knew it had to be worth a lot. Why else was that creepy Mr Bloodmoney so desperate to get his hands on it?

Slowly Debbie made a plan – she would give the lamp as a birthday present to her mum.

Then they could take it to an antique dealer to be valued. And then... She began to imagine how they could spend all that lovely money.

But first of all she had to polish it up a bit. She grabbed a rag and began to rub the lamp.

There was a sound like thunder, and a flash of light. The kitchen filled with smoke and there was a smell like old socks and kippers.

As soon as the smoke cleared,
Debbie saw with a shock that she was
not alone any more. An odd-looking
man was standing in
the kitchen.

He wore a suit and tie.
(That wasn't so odd.)
He had neat hair and
carried a briefcase.
(That wasn't very strange either.)
He was bright green, and he was so
tall his head nearly bumped the
ceiling. (Now THAT was a bit peculiar.)

Debbie was too stunned to speak. She opened and closed her mouth, but no sound came out.

But Debbie was not the kind of girl to stay stunned for very long.

'What did you expect?' said the genie. 'This IS the twenty-first century, isn't it? A genie can follow fashion too, you know. But you're right – maybe this IS a little formal.'

He clicked his fingers – SNAP! – and he was wearing a T-shirt and jeans.

The genie shook his head impatiently.

'Not any more. The Genies' Union voted to scrap that system… oh, two hundred years ago. It wasn't working out. We weren't happy in our jobs, the wishers weren't satisfied with the service. So we started a new system for wishes.'

Which is?

The owner of the lamp can make any wish within a period of two hours. After that, I return to the lamp.

Now, if I can just explain the other rules…

Debbie's mind was racing. Just think of all the things she could get... But the clock was ticking! Only two hours!

She said quickly, 'That's okay, don't worry about the details. Now did you say "any wish"? So, for example, if I say I want... a million pounds...'

'Very well,' sighed the genie, sounding rather bored. He clicked his fingers and... nothing happened.

The genie sniffed like a snooty waiter in a restaurant. He said, 'Well *what*? I suppose you expected a big treasure chest full of gold coins? We don't do things that way any more. Look in your pocket.'

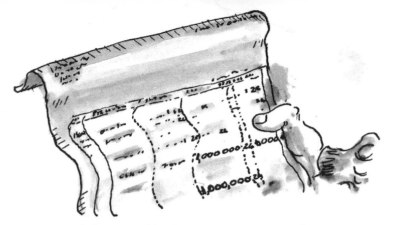

Debbie pulled out a piece of paper. It was a bank statement and it was in her name.

'One million pounds, and twenty-four pence,' she read aloud.

'The twenty-four pence was already in your account,' explained the genie coolly.

Debbie grinned and rubbed her hands together. It was time to get down to business...

4

A surprise for Vicky

When Vicky finished her paper round, she thought at first she was going crazy. The street looked the same as ever, except for their little house... It was gone! In its place stood a huge palace. It had a row of white pillars at the front, and two stone lions guarded the front door.

In a daze, Vicky went up the path. The garden – which used to have a birdbath and a rusty old swing – now looked like the gardens of a palace.

The hedges were trimmed into perfect animal shapes. A herd of white horses grazed in the meadows beyond.

Inside the house, it was even more amazing – the floors were the finest marble and beautiful paintings hung on every wall. There was gold everywhere, and the hallway led to the biggest double staircase she had ever seen.

In the kitchen Vicky found Kenny
Noggles – Debbie's favourite pop star –
gobbling caviar out of a cereal bowl.

She wandered open-mouthed
through what had once been the
dining room. It was an indoor
Olympic-size swimming pool now.

At last she found Debbie in the
living room.

Seeing that giant green face was the
last straw for Vicky. She fell backwards
in a dead faint.

When she woke up again, the same green face was looming over her. It hadn't been a bad dream. Her sister was beaming at her.

What's going on?

Promise not to faint again?

Vicky nodded, and Debbie began to explain all about the genie and the lamp.

There's one thing I don't understand. Why don't the neighbours think it's funny that we're suddenly millionaires living in a palace?

Debbie just tapped her head and winked.

Already thought of it, sis. I wished that no one round here would notice any of the changes.

Vicky gulped. She was just beginning to realize that it was all real.

So what else did you wish for?

Oh, the usual stuff. Fabulous riches, success and good health... all that stuff. Mum and Dad'll be surprised, won't they?

Vicky was too shocked to reply.

I guess you were wrong, sis— Sometimes you **CAN** get something for nothing. All these wishes cost nothing!

She grinned and waved at all the splendid things around them.

And that's when things began to go wrong...

5

Deep trouble

The genie leaned forward and gave a polite cough.

Ahem. I couldn't help overhearing... but did you say 'nothing'?

Debbie got a horrible feeling deep in her stomach. This didn't sound like good news. She nodded.

I'm afraid that's not true. I was trying to explain everything to you earlier—but you decided not to hear me out. The Genies' Union have changed the rules of wishing.

Yes, I know. I wish for two hours and then you go back to the lamp.

The genie raised one eyebrow.

He said, 'But that's not all. You didn't let me tell you the other changes. The Genies' Union has just decided that we should be paid for what we do. Why should we go around granting wishes for free? And so at the end of each two-hour period, the wisher is now given a bill.'

The truth hit Debbie like a speeding train.

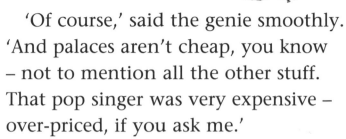

A bill? You mean... I've got to pay for all this?

'Of course,' said the genie smoothly. 'And palaces aren't cheap, you know – not to mention all the other stuff. That pop singer was very expensive – over-priced, if you ask me.'

Vicky shook her head. Her little sister was in deep trouble.

So what's the bill?

The genie clicked his fingers, and a long bill appeared in the air. A VERY long bill.

Debbie felt as if she couldn't breathe.
A desperate idea leapt into her mind.

Hold on! What if I wish for enough money to pay the bill?

'It won't work,' said Vicky. 'You'd have to pay for the money you wished for, as well as all the other stuff.'

'Plus interest,' added the genie.

Panic tightened its grip on Debbie. Was there no way out?

The genie looked business-like. 'There is another way, of course, to pay the bill. You can work it off in one of the factories where we have all the wish items built.'

He glanced again at the bill and pulled out a pocket calculator from thin air.

Now, let me see. It should only take you... twelve thousand, eight hundred and sixty-two years to pay this off – plus a few days.

'That's impossible!' gasped Vicky, but Debbie just shook her head sadly.

The genie gave his 'snooty waiter'
sniff again.

Debbie looked glumly at her new, solid-gold, diamond-studded watch. Only forty minutes before the two hours were up. What could she do?

Then Vicky spoke up.

For the first time she sounded like her usual, bossy self again.

6

Against the rules

Time was running out, but Vicky
skimmed through the copy of the
rules as quickly as she could. The print
was tiny, and she had to squint and
hold her head right next to the paper
to read it.

At first it looked hopeless. There
didn't seem to be any way out. The
wisher was not allowed to wish
that the past two hours had never
happened, or anything like that. But
then...

'If the owner sells the lamp to another person (not including the person from whom she or he bought the lamp) within the two hours, then the wishes made shall become null and void, and the contract terminated.'

Debbie scratched her head.

'Don't you get it?' cried Vicky. 'If you sell the lamp before the two hours are up, then all of the wishes will disappear and you won't have to pay. But you can't sell it back to the shop, and

you've only got... twenty minutes! The only thing is, who could you sell it to?'

It hit Debbie in a flash.

Bloodmoney! Bloodmoney knows about the lamp – but he doesn't know EVERYTHING about it.

Debbie told her sister how Bloodmoney had tried to get the lamp from her.

> Bloodmoney, hmm.

Debbie turned to the genie.

> Genie, can you take me to Charles Bloodmoney?

The genie shook his head stiffly. 'It's against the rules, I'm afraid. Clause 91, Section C. *No wishes may be used to find a new buyer.* I cannot do *anything* to help you find a new buyer.'

'No need!' cried Vicky. 'I've seen that name before. I've seen it on a gate, on my paper round. It's that big house, up on Roundley Hill.'

Debbie jumped up.

He seemed to shimmer and
turn to smoke. Then he shot up
the spout and into the lamp.

She scooped up the lamp and
charged outside to her bike.

7

A race against time

Debbie cycled like never before. She pushed down on the pedals with all her might. The genie's lamp rattled in the front basket. On she rode.

Fifteen minutes to go… don't stop now! she thought to herself.

She turned sharp left and felt the wind hit her head on. She gritted her teeth and forced her legs to push harder, to go faster. She zoomed down hills and she puffed and panted up hills. On she rode.

Ten minutes to go… keep going!…
nine minutes…

A dog jumped out at her, barking furiously. She nearly fell off, but she managed to keep her balance and keep going. On she rode.

Eight minutes until time was up…
would she make it?

Debbie was on the road that led to Bloodmoney's house now. Her legs ached, but she never slowed down. Her heart pounded, *baDUM, baDUM, baDUM*. The pedals whirred under her.

Five minutes…

At last she reached the drive-way!
She zoomed up the gravel path
and leapt off her bike. She pressed
the doorbell…

and waited…

… and waited.

No reply.
Was anyone in? Would anyone ever
come to the door?

Two minutes to go…

The door
opened a crack
and Bloodmoney's
thin face peered
out.

When he saw Debbie with the lamp
his eyes gleamed like a wolf spotting
its supper.

'I've changed my mind!' gasped
Debbie. 'You can have the lamp!'

Bloodmoney was greedy to have the
lamp, but he was not stupid. His cold
eyes narrowed in suspicion.

He said, '*Why* have you changed your
mind? And how did you find me?'

Debbie's mind raced frantically. She pointed at the giant car that was parked in the driveway.

She gasped, 'I knew you lived here 'cause I saw the car. And I want to sell the lamp because I didn't realize it was all bashed about. Look, it's got a big dent on one side.'

She held the lamp up for him to see and thought to herself, *PLEASE BELIEVE ME! I'M NEARLY OUT OF TIME!*

'And you noticed nothing unusual about the lamp?' asked Bloodmoney sharply.

Debbie shook her head. She pretended not to see the sparkle of greed in his eye.

Hmm, as it's got a dent, I'll give you... five pounds for it.

Debbie did not hesitate.

Done!

Bloodmoney dug a bony hand into his pocket and tossed a five pound note to her. Then he snatched the lamp and slammed the door shut.

SLAM

SLAM

Debbie looked down at the money in her hand – five whole pounds. She grinned.

Good luck, Mr Bloodmoney... I think you'll need it!

8

After it all

The next day Debbie and Vicky were walking back from school. Everything was back to normal. All the things Debbie had wished for were gone. The genie had done his work well and no one remembered that anything unusual had ever happened. The genie had even made *Vicky* forget all about it.

Only Debbie knew the truth.

So what are you going to get Mum for her birthday?

'Dunno,' said Debbie. 'I've got five pounds I wasn't expecting. Maybe I'll get a craft book out of the library and make her something. After all, it's the thought that counts.'

They came to the newsagent's.

'Time for my paper round,' said Vicky. 'Oh hey, I meant to tell you – they need another person for the morning paper round. Are you interested?'

For a moment, Debbie almost said 'yes'. *Almost.* But then she thought of how nice it was to snuggle up in bed in the morning, and how rotten it must be to trudge through the wind and rain carrying a sackful of newspapers.

We'll see.

About the author

When I was growing up
in Manchester, I always
wanted to be an
astronaut, a footballer,
or (if those didn't work
out for any reason)
perhaps a rock star. So it
came as something of a
shock when I became
first a teacher and then an editor
of educational books.

I have lived in Cambridge, Aylesbury,
Oxford and Istanbul. I'm still on the run and
now live in Chicago with my wife and family.

There is a real Debbie I know, and the
Debbie in this story is based on her!